EMOTIONAL INTELLIGENCE

Developing Essential Skills
for Success in Life and Work

Dr. Donald J. Henry

TABLE OF CONTENTS

DISCLAIMER

BOOK DESCRIPTION

The title of the book is "Emotional Intelligence: Developing Essential Skills for Success in Life and Work" Creating Fundamental Abilities for Outcome Throughout everyday life and Work.
You will be able to succeed in both your personal and professional lives if you read this captivating book, which is your key to mastering the art of emotional intelligence. Plan to leave on an extraordinary excursion that will hoist how you might interpret feelings and prepare for a satisfying and prosperous future.

You will learn how emotional intelligence has a significant impact on every aspect of your life in this compelling guide. Dive into the five centre parts of the capacity to understand individuals on a deeper level mindfulness, self-guideline, inspiration, compassion, and interactive abilities, and figure out how to bridle their ability to accomplish your objectives, fabricate significant connections, and explore life's difficulties with certainty.

Do you want to work in a more harmonious environment where people work well together and communicate well? Look no further. "Emotional Intelligence" unwinds the complexities of compassionate correspondence, compromise, and successful initiative, changing you into a significant resource in your expert undertakings.

Do you want to deepen your connections with other people and improve your relationships? This book's accommodating tone and engaging tales make it an inspiring excursion of self-revelation and sympathy. By fostering your capacity to understand individuals at their core, you'll manufacture significant associations with people around you, enhancing your connections and leaving an enduring effect.

Find how the ability to appreciate people on a profound level can be supported in kids and youngsters, forming the heads of tomorrow with close-to-home insight and compassion. As a parent or educator, you have the authority to lead the younger generation toward emotional resilience and personal development, preparing them for a bright and compassionate future.

"Emotional Intelligence: Developing Essential Skills for Success in Life and Work" isn't simply one more self-improvement guide; a complete and reasonable aide outfits you with the instruments to change your life. Embrace the insight of the capacity to understand individuals on a profound level, and you'll open the way to a more satisfied, deliberate, and effective presence.

Why purchase this book? because it serves as a compass that will direct you toward thriving relationships and emotional empowerment. Since it's an interest in your self-improvement and expert achievement because it demonstrates the transformative potential of emotion management.

You'll be captivated by the profound impact that emotional intelligence can have on your life with every page-turn. Thus, if you're prepared to set out on a groundbreaking excursion towards an all the more genuinely smart and satisfied future, "The Capacity to understand people on a deeper level: The Book, "Developing Essential Skills for Success in Life and Work," will lead you there. Don't pass up this chance to sail toward success, connection, and meaning in life. Get your duplicate now and embrace the excursion of the ability to appreciate people on a profound level.

INTRODUCTION

THE POWER OF EMOTIONAL INTELLIGENCE

The significance of emotional intelligence has risen to the vanguard of private and expert achievement withinside the fast moving global we stay in. A collection of essential skills that enable individuals to effectively recognize, comprehend, and manage their emotions, as well as to navigate interpersonal relationships with empathy and compassion, is known as emotional intelligence, or EQ.

Understanding Emotional Intelligence and Its Impact Self-awareness, or a thorough understanding of one's emotions, triggers, and behaviour patterns, is the foundation of emotional intelligence. People can develop emotional regulation through this self-awareness, which enables them to handle difficult situations with poise and composure.

Also, the capacity to appreciate individuals at their core stretches out past mindfulness; it includes the ability to feel for other people, see their feelings, and answer with awareness and understanding. Emotional intelligence is a powerful force that encourages open communication and harmonious relationships thanks to its unique combination of interpersonal and intrapersonal skills.

The Numerous Benefits of Developing Emotional Intelligence in Life and Work Developing emotional intelligence can result in a plethora of advantages that enhance both personal and professional life. Emotional intelligence enables individuals to cultivate a deeper sense of understanding and trust within relationships, resulting in stronger personal connections with loved ones. It gives people the ability to handle conflicts with grace, which makes connections healthier and more fulfilling.

In the domain of work, the capacity to understand people on a deeper level is an impetus for successful administration and group coordinated effort. Pioneers with high EQ move and persuade their groups, establishing a positive and steady workplace. In addition, the ability to appreciate people on a profound level upgrades correspondence and compromise, considering more strong and useful groups.

All through this excursion, we will investigate the complexities of the ability to appreciate anyone on a deeper level and divulge pragmatic ways of raising your EQ. From creating mindfulness and profound guidelines to encouraging compassion and dominating interactive abilities, every section will give noteworthy stages to improve your capacity to understand anyone on a deeper level and open your maximum capacity for outcome throughout everyday life and work.

Embrace the force of the capacity to understand people on a deeper level, and set out on a groundbreaking excursion that will engage you to explore feelings, make bona fide associations, and cultivate significant connections. Let its profound impact illuminate your path to a life filled with fulfilment, resilience, and emotional wisdom as we delve into the depths of emotional intelligence.

Chapter 1

Five Components of Emotional Intelligence

The capacity to understand people on a profound level **(EQ)** is a diverse range of abilities that frames the foundation of successful relational connections and self-improvement. In this part, we will investigate the five fundamental parts of the ability to understand people on a deeper level and their significant effect on our lives.

1. Self-Awareness: Perceiving and Figuring out Your Feelings

Mindfulness lays the foundation for the capacity to appreciate individuals on a deeper level. By fostering sharp identity mindfulness, we can distinguish and figure out our feelings, perceiving their triggers and examples. We can respond to situations with greater insight and authenticity as a result of our increased self-awareness, resulting in better emotional regulation and decision-making based on information.

2. Self-Regulation: Dealing with Feelings Really

Self-guideline is the specialty of dealing with our feelings successfully, even notwithstanding affliction. By developing a self-guideline, we gain the ability to answer testing circumstances with poise and restriction. We can improve our emotional well-being by developing emotional resilience and avoiding impulsive responses through a variety of methods and practices.

3. Motivation: Directing Feelings to Drive Objectives and Desires

The ability to appreciate people on a profound level energizes our inspiration, permitting us to tackle our feelings to drive us toward our objectives and desires. With an unmistakable comprehension of what drives us, we can remain on track and decide in any event, when confronted with obstructions. This part of the capacity to understand individuals on a deeper level fills in as a directing power on our excursion to progress and satisfaction.

4. Empathy: Creating Understanding and Empathy for Other people

Compassion is the extension that interfaces us to others on a more profound level. By creating sympathy, we can see and figure out the feelings of others, cultivating empathy and real association. Through undivided attention and a certifiable craving to comprehend others' points of view, we can sustain significant and strong connections.

5. Social abilities: Fostering Strong Relationships and Effective Communication

The final part of emotional intelligence is a set of social skills that help us navigate relationships and communicate well. By dominating interactive abilities, we can fabricate trust, resolve clashes, and team up agreeably. Whether in a personal or professional setting, these abilities are crucial for creating a welcoming and encouraging social environment.

All through this section, we will dig into every part of the capacity to understand people on a profound level, giving viable activities and experiences to assist you with upgrading your EQ. Let your understanding and growth of emotional intelligence serve as your compass as you embark on this journey of self-discovery toward a life that is more satisfying and harmonious.

With every part, you will open the keys to profound insight, sympathy, and legitimate association, engaging you to explore feelings with beauty and compassion, both inside yourself and in your associations with others.

Chapter 2

Assessing Your Emotional Intelligence

Similarly, as a mariner checks out their boat before heading out, it's fundamental to evaluate our capacity to understand individuals on a profound level before setting out on our excursion of self-revelation. In this chapter, we'll look at how to assess your emotional intelligence, find your strengths, and figure out where you can improve. By focusing light on your close-to-home scene, you'll acquire significant bits of knowledge that will fuel your self-improvement and advancement.

Recognizing Your Strengths and Areas for Improvement
Your emotional intelligence is like a treasure chest filled with hidden strengths. Understanding your assets enables you to use them in exploring life's difficulties and building satisfying connections.

There may be areas that could benefit from development and nurturing alongside these strengths. Recognizing these regions sets out opens doors for personal development, upgrading your capacity to appreciate anyone at their core over the long haul.

Agreeable Tip: Keep a diary where you ponder your profound reactions and cooperation with others. Observe minutes when your capacity to understand people on a profound level sparkles and when there's space for development. This mindfulness will direct your excursion of progress.

Devices for Surveying and Estimating The ability to appreciate people at their core The capacity to appreciate people on a deeper level excursion turns out to be considerably more remunerating when you have navigational devices available to you. To accurately measure emotional intelligence, numerous assessment tools and approaches have been developed. By utilizing these devices, you can acquire a more profound comprehension of your close-to-home qualities and regions that could utilize some sustaining.

1. **Self-Evaluation Polls**
Answer intriguing inquiries regarding your feelings, ways of behaving, and interactive abilities to check your capacity to appreciate anyone at their core.

2. **360-Degree Evaluation**
Find out how your trusted friends, family, or coworkers feel about your emotional intelligence in various situations.

3. **Tests of Emotional Intelligence**
Take tests that have been scientifically designed to measure various aspects of emotional intelligence to get complete information.

A Helpful Tip: Recall that evaluations are not marks but instead guideposts on your excursion. Accept the criticism with an open heart, recognize your strengths, and view areas of improvement as opportunities for growth.

Keep in mind that this evaluation of your emotional intelligence is an ongoing journey as you begin it. The capacity to understand individuals on a deeper level isn't an objective, but instead a journey of persistent development and revelation. Comment on the headway you make and the bits of knowledge acquired, realizing that each step carries you more like a daily existence loaded up with profound insight and versatility.

You can unlock the potential to make connections with other people that are real and meaningful by taking an emotional intelligence test. This will give you a better understanding of who you are. Together, we should head out on this groundbreaking excursion, exploring feelings, encouraging mindfulness, and embracing the force of the capacity to understand individuals on a profound level to lead a satisfying and amicable life.

Chapter 3

Cultivating Self-Awareness

In the tremendous ocean of the capacity to understand people on a deeper level, mindfulness fills in as the directing North Star, a guide that enlightens the profundities of our feelings and inward world. In this part, we'll leave on an extraordinary excursion of developing mindfulness, plunging into the significant significance of care in figuring out feelings and investigating procedures to rehearse self-reflection and profound mindfulness.

The Significance of Care in Grasping Feelings

Care resembles a beacon that keeps us moored right now, assisting us explore the turbulent rushes of our feelings with clearness and presence. By rehearsing care, we can notice our feelings as they emerge, without judgement or connection. We become more self-aware as a result of this profound sense of presence, which enables us to comprehend the ups and downs of our emotional tides.

Helpful Tip: Set aside a few minutes each day for mindfulness meditation or engage in fully present activities like mindful eating and walking to incorporate mindfulness into your daily routine. These snapshots of care encourage a more profound comprehension of your feelings as they emerge over the day.

Self-reflection and emotional awareness can be practiced in a variety of ways. Think of self-reflection as a ship's telescope, a tool that lets you focus on your emotions and learn about their underlying causes and triggers. Through self-reflection, you can explore your close-to-home scene, looking at the underlying foundations of your sentiments and responses. You can develop emotional awareness and a stronger connection to your emotions through this practice.

1. Journaling: Keep a diary to record your considerations, sentiments, and encounters. Ordinary journaling offers a place of refuge for self-articulation and profound investigation.

2. Mapping Emotions: Make a visual portrayal of your feelings, utilising varieties and images to portray various sentiments and their powers. This procedure improves close-to-home mindfulness and assists you with spotting designs.

3. Focused Body Scan: You can perform a mindful body scan by carefully observing every part of your body and identifying any areas of tension or discomfort. This training encourages familiarity with how feelings manifest genuinely.

4. Emotional Monitoring Every Day: Put away a couple of seconds every day to genuinely check in with yourself. Ask yourself how you're feeling, what feelings emerge, and what occasions or circumstances might have set off them.

Helpful Tip: Be delicate and sympathetic with yourself during self-reflection. Understanding emotions can sometimes be difficult due to their complexity. Embrace every understanding with consideration, realising that close-to-home mindfulness is an expertise that develops with training.

As you develop mindfulness, recollect that there's no need to focus on examining or passing judgement on your feelings yet on embracing them with open interest. Developing mindfulness is a journey of self-disclosure and self-awareness.

Through mindfulness and self-reflection, you can illuminate your emotional landscape and develop the emotional intelligence necessary to face life's challenges with greater wisdom and resilience. Together, we should set out on this extraordinary excursion, embracing mindfulness as the compass that guides us toward profound genuineness and understanding.

Chapter 4

Mastering Self-Regulation

Self-regulation enables us to navigate the turbulent waters of our emotions with finesse and composure, much like a skilled captain who steers their ship through turbulent waters. In this part, we'll dig into the craft of dominating self-guideline, investigating viable procedures for overseeing pressure and close-to-home reactivity. We'll likewise find feeling guideline methods that prepare for a reasonable and agreeable reaction to life's difficulties.

Techniques for Overseeing Pressure and Close Home Reactivity
Life's journey isn't without its tempests, and stress frequently lingers not too far off like violent waves. When we face challenges, self-regulation serves as an anchor that keeps us grounded. We can prevent stress from becoming overwhelming and triggering emotional reactivity by effectively managing it.

1. Breathing in Mind: Practice profound, careful breathing when stress emerges. Centre around your breath to focus yourself and make a feeling of quiet amid the tempest.

2. Time-Outs: When you're feeling overwhelmed, take a few short breaks. Moving back from an upsetting circumstance gives time for feelings to settle, permitting you to answer all the more objectively.

3. coping strategies: Foster sound survival techniques to manage pressure, like activity, side interests, or investing energy in nature.

Helpful Tip: Keep in mind that it's alright to ask for help from other people during stressful times. Discussing your thoughts with a believed companion or relative can give solace and assist you with acquiring a viewpoint.

Feeling Guideline Procedures for a Reasonable Reaction
Feelings can once in a while resemble tempestuous oceans, taking steps to overturn our profound boat. The art of stabilising our vessels and encouraging a balanced response to our emotions is known as emotion regulation.

1. Identify the Causes: Perceive the circumstances or occasions that trigger extraordinary feelings, empowering you to carefully get ready for and answer them.

2. Positive Rethinking: Rethink pessimistic contemplations into additional positive and useful points of view, moving your profound reaction towards confidence.

3. Communicating Feelings Securely: Track down solid ways of communicating your feelings, like through journaling, imaginative outlets, or discussions with figuring out companions.

4. Developing Compassion: Develop compassion towards yourself as well as other people, perceiving that feelings are a characteristic piece of being human.

A helpful tip: Take your time as you learn to control your emotions. It takes practice to master emotional waters, just like sailing.

As you ace self-guideline, you oversee your close-to-home sails, permitting you to explore life's difficulties with balance and poise. Self-guideline isn't tied in with stifling feelings however about overseeing them in a solid and adjusted way.

By applying pressure to the executives' methodologies and feeling guideline procedures, you'll make a strong and quiet profound ocean inside yourself. Together, how about we lift the banner of self-guideline high, embracing this enabling ability as the breeze in our sails, directing us towards close-to-home concordance and internal strength?

Chapter 5

Igniting Motivation from Within

In the same way that a strong wind fills a ship's sails, igniting motivation from within propels us forward on our journey toward personal growth and fulfilment. The essence of igniting intrinsic motivation and passion, as well as the art of setting meaningful goals and remaining resilient in the face of unpredictability, will be the focus of this chapter.

Finding Characteristic Inspirations and Enthusiasm
Characteristic inspiration is the delicate current that runs profoundly inside us, driving us towards exercises and pursuits that give us pleasure and satisfaction. Uncovering our natural inspirations permits us to diagram a course lined up with our interests and values, making a feeling of direction on our excursion.

Helpful Tip: Make time for reflection and self-exploration. Consider the exercises that cause you to forget about time and fill you with energy. These are the murmurs of your natural inspirations directing you toward your actual interests.

Defining Significant Objectives and Keeping Up with Versatility
Like making a plan on a navigational graph, defining significant objectives steers us toward our ideal objective. At the point when we put forth objectives that reverberate with our inborn inspirations, we become like decided mariners, overflowing with strength and assurance.

1. Smart Targets: Set Explicit, Quantifiable, Attainable, Important, and Time-Bound objectives. Savvy objectives give an unmistakable heading and substantial achievements to pursue.

2. Step-by-Step Goal Setting: Break down larger objectives into manageable steps. Your motivation will increase with each step completed.

3. Embracing Flexibility: We may face difficulties and storms in the sea of life, but resilience enables us to recover and maintain our course. Embrace mishaps as learning amazing open doors, and track down strength even with misfortune.

Helpful Tip: Celebrate your progress every step of the way, even the smallest ones. Celebrations keep you motivated and help you remember how far you've come.

As you light inspiration from the inside, you become the skipper of your boat, directing toward a reason-driven life. By adjusting your excursion to your inborn interests and putting forth significant objectives, you tackle the breezes of inspiration to push you forward.

Embrace strength as your anchor, keeping you resolute during testing times. Together, we should head out with the compass of inborn inspiration, diagramming a course that prompts an existence of enthusiasm, reason, and relentless assurance.

Chapter 6

Developing Empathy and Compassion

We navigate the waters of emotional intelligence, developing empathy and compassion becomes the star that guides our relationships with others. Through active listening and empathetic responses, we will embark on a transformative journey to comprehend the viewpoint of others and investigate the art of enhancing empathy.

Figuring out the Point of View of Others
Envision venturing onto the deck of someone else's boat, seeing the world through their eyes. Empathy is the compass that leads us on this journey, allowing us to comprehend and empathise with other people's feelings and experiences.
By venturing beyond ourselves and seeing the world from their vantage point, we cultivate certified associations and empathy.

Helpful Tip: Practice viewpoint-taking in your day-to-day connections. Try to picture yourself in the person's position as you listen to their story. This training improves your capacity to understand their feelings.

Enhancing Empathy Through Active Listening and Empathetic Responses
Active listening is like setting sail with a keen ear. It enables us to understand and pay attention to the emotional currents in a conversation. We give the speaker our full attention by fully engaging in active listening and validating their feelings and experiences.

1. focus: Set aside interruptions and spotlight the individual talking. Visually engage and show authentic interest in what they're talking about.

2. Sympathetic Reactions: Answer with compassion and understanding, recognizing their sentiments and approving their encounters. "I understand," "That must have been difficult," or "I can see why you feel that way" are all good examples.

3. Pose Unrestricted Questions: By asking open-ended questions, you can encourage the speaker to talk more. This shows that you are intrigued by their viewpoint.

Helpful Tip: Being a supportive presence rather than offering solutions or solving problems is the essence of empathy. Simply being there to listen and comprehend can sometimes be the most meaningful response.

You become a bridge that connects hearts and fosters genuine connections with others as you develop empathy and compassion. Sympathy is the anchor that keeps us grounded in the force of understanding and empathy.

By effectively tuning in and answering sympathetically, you make a climate of trust and receptiveness in your connections. Together, we should explore the waters of sympathy, encouraging further associations and developing a world loaded up with empathy and understanding.

Chapter 7

Nurturing Social Skills and Emotional Intelligence

In Relationships

As we navigate the waters of emotional intelligence, developing our social skills become the compass that helps us make connections that matter and build relationships that work well together. In this section, we'll investigate the craft of building entrust and profound associations with others and dive into the significance of powerful correspondence for solid relational connections.

Building Trust and Profound Association with Others
Envision the connections between people's areas of strength as that anchor delivers together. Building trust and profound association is the most common way of winding around these ropes, making a feeling that everything is safe and secure, and grasping our connections. Trust frames the bedrock of any relationship, taking into consideration weakness and profound closeness.

1. Consistency and Unwavering quality: Be trustworthy and consistent in your words and actions. As a result, you'll develop a sense of dependability and build trust in your relationships.

2. Understanding and compassion: Validate the feelings and perspectives of others and demonstrate empathy for their experiences and emotions. This fosters deeper comprehension and emotional connection.

3. Vulnerability and Transparency: Sincerely share your thoughts and feelings so that others can see you for who you are. Openness fosters deeper emotional bonds and reciprocation.

Helpful Tip: Trust is worked over the long haul through steady activities and basic encouragement. Be patient, and permit connections to normally create.

Communication is the wind that blows relationships into understanding and mutual respect. Effective communication is essential for healthy interpersonal relationships. Compelling correspondence is the craft of communicating one's thoughts obviously and tuning in with an open heart.

1. Undivided attention: Engage in conversations fully and give the speaker your full attention. Listen to understand as well as respond.

2. Clear and Confident Articulation: Use "I" statements to express your point of view and communicate your thoughts and feelings clearly and assertively, avoiding blaming or judging others.

3. Compromise: Conflicts should be seen as opportunities for learning and understanding. Look to settle on something worth agreeing on and split the difference, as opposed to zeroing in on being correct.

Helpful Tip: Keep in mind that speaking and listening are two aspects of communication. Empower open exchange and make a place of refuge for legitimate articulation in your connections.

As you support interactive abilities and the capacity to understand people on a profound level in your connections, you become a talented guide of the close-to-home waters, cultivating significant associations and building agreeable bonds with others.

Building trust and close-to-home association establishes the groundwork for legitimate and satisfying connections, while successful correspondence guarantees going great in the oceans of understanding.

Embracing the power of social skills and emotional intelligence to create a world enriched with love, empathy, and meaningful relationships, let's sail together toward the horizon of heartfelt connections.

Chapter 8

Emotional Intelligence in the Workplace

As we explore the expert waters, the capacity to appreciate people on a deeper level turns into the directing compass that shapes our outcome in the working environment. In this section, we'll investigate the force of utilising the capacity to understand people on a profound level for compelling administration and dig into its importance in group elements and cooperation.

Utilising The ability to understand individuals at their core for Compelling Authority

In the domain of authority, the capacity to understand people on a profound level goes about as the skipper's rudder, controlling the boat toward an agreeable and useful working environment. Pioneers who tackle the ability to appreciate people on a profound level move and inspire their groups, establishing a climate where representatives flourish and arrive at their maximum capacity.

1. Understanding and compassion: Compelling pioneers show compassion and understanding towards their colleagues' feelings and requirements, encouraging a strong and caring work culture.

2. Close to home Guideline: Pioneers with the capacity to understand individuals on a deeper level control their feelings, answering difficulties with poise and keeping a good work air.

3. Trust and Integrity: Pioneers who are credible and straightforward form entrust with their groups, encouraging devotion and responsibility.

Helpful Tip: Authority isn't tied in with applying control yet about enabling and moving others. Embrace worker administration, focusing on the prosperity and development of your group.

Emotional Intelligence and Team Dynamics and Collaboration Picture a workplace where employees collaborate like sailors, each contributing to the ship's success. Effective collaboration and cooperation among team members is facilitated by emotional intelligence in team dynamics.

1. Emotional Intelligence: Colleagues who are sincerely mindful grasp their feelings and perceive the feelings of their partners, prompting better correspondence and compromise.

2. Sympathetic Correspondence: Teams with high emotional intelligence engage in empathetic communication by actively listening to one another and responding in a manner that is both respectful and receptive.

3. Compromise: Emotional intelligence enables teams to resolve conflicts constructively, discover solutions that benefit all parties, and strengthen team ties.

Helpful Tip: Support open correspondence and make a place of refuge for communicating feelings inside your group. This cultivates a feeling of mental security and improves group elements.

As you embrace the capacity to understand people on a deeper level in the working environment, you become a gifted skipper, directing your group toward an effective and amicable journey. Utilising the capacity to understand individuals on a profound level as a pioneer encourages a positive workplace, improving representative confidence and efficiency.

In group elements, the capacity to appreciate people at their core makes a durable and cooperative team, cruising towards imparted objectives to sympathy and understanding. Together, we should tackle the influence of the capacity to understand people on a deeper level in the working environment, moving our associations towards success and making a culture enhanced with compassion, collaboration, and accomplishment.

Chapter 9

Overcoming Challenges and Embracing Growth

We explore the flighty waters of life, the ability to understand anyone on a deeper level turns into the raft that helps us through sincerely tough spots. We will look at how to deal with difficult situations and use emotional intelligence to not only survive but also thrive in adversity in this chapter.

Managing Sincerely Tough spots
Life isn't without its tempests, and inner challenges might emerge out of the blue. Be that as it may, with the capacity to understand people at their core as your anchor, you can explore these whirlwinds with strength and effortlessness.

1. Acknowledgment and Affirmation: Recognize your feelings without judgement, tolerating that encountering trouble and agony on occasion is ordinary.

2. Looking for Help: Make sure to get help from companions, family, or experts during genuinely testing times. The burden is lessened and your emotional resilience is strengthened when you share your feelings.

3. coping mechanisms: Foster sound survival methods that assist you with overseeing pressure and feelings, for example, care practices, working out, or participating in imaginative exercises.

Well-disposed Tip: Recollect that personal hardships are brief, and you have the solidarity to beat them. Be caring to yourself and approach slowly and carefully towards mending.

Using Emotional Intelligence to Thrive in Adversity Like a strong sail that catches the wind, emotional intelligence enables you to use adversity as an opportunity for growth and to weather the storm.

1. Profound Adaptability: Develop profound adaptability, permitting yourself to encounter a scope of feelings without getting overpowered.

2. Reframing Positively: Search for silver linings and examples in affliction, reexamining difficulties as any open doors for learning and self-improvement.

3. Strength and Flexibility: Embrace flexibility and versatility as your partners in exploring life's vulnerabilities, realising that you can quickly return and flourish.

Cordial Tip: Accept challenges as opportunities for learning and development. Each tough spot can be an impetus for individual change.

As you conquer difficulties and embrace development, you become the talented mariner who courageously explores the profound waters of life. With the ability to appreciate individuals on a deeper level as your compass, you steer towards close-to-home prosperity and flourishing flexibility.

Managing genuinely tough spots turns into an opportunity to sustain your capacity to understand individuals on a profound level and arise more grounded and savvier.

Let's sail toward emotional empowerment together, seeing difficulties as opportunities for development and discovery. You will rise higher with each challenge, not only overcoming obstacles but also accepting the journey of self-discovery and emotional fulfillment.

Chapter 10

Raising Emotional Intelligence In Children and Teens

The journey through the oceans of the ability to appreciate people on a deeper level, we find the meaning of encouraging the capacity to understand people on a deeper level in the more youthful age. In this part, we'll investigate the specialty of sustaining the capacity to understand people on a deeper level in instructive settings and dig into compelling nurturing procedures for creating the ability to appreciate individuals on a deeper level in kids and teenagers.

Education as a Safe Haven for the Development of Emotional Intelligence Picture educational settings as fertile ground for the development of emotional intelligence in young minds. Instructors and teachers assume an essential part in cultivating the capacity to understand people on a profound level in schools and homerooms.

1. Close-to-home Training: Incorporate close-to-home schooling into the educational plan, helping kids to distinguish and figure out their feelings and those of others.

2. Interactive abilities Preparing: Set out open doors for interactive abilities preparing, empowering coordinated effort, compassion, and powerful correspondence among understudies.

3. Everyday encouragement: Offer everyday reassurance to understudies, establishing a mindful climate where they have a good sense of security to communicate their sentiments and concerns.

Amicable Tip: Integrate the ability to appreciate individuals on a profound level into different exercises, for example, narrating, pretending, and conversations, to make learning pleasant and locking in.

Strategies for Developing Emotional Intelligence as a Parent Parents become the guiding lights, encouraging their children's emotional intelligence from the very beginning of their journey.

1. Positive Examples: Be a personal good example for your youngsters, telling them the best way to communicate feelings successfully and oversee them in solid ways.

2. Close-to-home Instructing: Practice close-to-home training by effectively paying attention to your kid's sentiments and aiding them to mark and grasp their feelings.

3. Skills for Solving Problems: Show critical thinking abilities to your youngsters, engaging them to track down valuable answers for personal difficulties.

Cordial Tip: Establish an open and steady climate at home, where feelings are embraced and approved. Support open correspondence and compassion inside the family.

As you centre around bringing the ability to understand anyone on a profound level up in kids and teenagers, you become the directing beacon that enlightens their close-to-home excursion. In instructive settings, the ability to appreciate people on a profound level turns into a fundamental component of sustaining balanced and genuinely versatile people.

Nurturing techniques that stress everyday encouragement and sympathy establish the groundwork for kids to major areas of strength for fostering insight, engaging them to cruise without hesitation through the tempests and quiet waters of life. Let's work together to develop the younger generation's emotional intelligence by pointing them in the direction of emotional empowerment and preparing them for a life filled with insight, compassion, and wisdom.

Chapter 11

Integrating Emotional Intelligence In Your Life

We are close to the furthest limit of our groundbreaking journey, now is the ideal time to moor the illustrations of the capacity to understand anyone on a profound level immovably into our regular routines. In this section, we'll investigate the craft of coordinating capacity to understand people on a profound level into each part of our reality, making an activity plan for proceeding with development, and supporting the ability to understand individuals at their core for long-haul achievement.

Making an Activity Plan for Proceeded with Development

Like a carefully prepared mariner planning their excursion, making an activity plan for the capacity to understand individuals on a profound level guarantees that we keep on track and keep on developing.

1. Self-Reflection: Participate in standard self-reflection to distinguish areas of the ability to understand anyone at their core that you need to fortify and move along.

2. Set Smart Objectives: Set explicit, quantifiable, reachable, applicable, and time-headed objectives for your ability to understand anyone at their core improvement.

3. Daily Activities: To develop emotional intelligence, incorporate daily practices like mindfulness, self-awareness exercises, and empathetic communication.

4. Look for opportunities to learn: Go to studios, read books, or take seminars on the capacity to appreciate individuals at their core to extend your comprehension and abilities.

Helpful Tip: Show restraint toward yourself as you incorporate the ability to understand people on a deeper level into your life. It's a consistent excursion of development and learning.

Maintaining Emotional Intelligence for Long-Term Success Similar to the winds that propel us forward, maintaining emotional intelligence ensures that our progress and growth are maintained.

1. Implementation Consistency: Make your emotional intelligence practices an integral part of your daily routine to maintain consistency.

2. Close-to-home Registrations: Routinely check in with your feelings and profound reactions, guaranteeing that you stay receptive to your close-to-home scene.

3. Consider Progress: Ponder your ability to appreciate people at their core process, praising your development and perceiving regions where you have space to create.

4. Embrace Backing: Rest with the help of companions, family, or tutors who can support and guide you on your capacity to appreciate individuals on a deeper level excursion.

Amicable Tip: A lifelong skill that can always be improved upon is emotional intelligence. Accept the constant growth and development process.

You become the captain of your emotional ship as you incorporate emotional intelligence into your life, steering it toward a life that is more satisfying and harmonious. Maintaining emotional intelligence ensures that you can face life's challenges with wisdom and resilience, and creating an action plan for continued growth keeps you on track.

Together, how about we anchor the ability to appreciate people on a deeper level in our souls and psyches, embracing the force of figuring out, compassion, and mindfulness? With each new day, you'll head out towards an all the more sincerely savvy and satisfying life, enabled to explore feelings with beauty and embrace the excursion of self-revelation and self-awareness.

CONCLUSION

Embrace The Journey of Emotional Intelligence

Everything has begining and end as we reach the finish of this extraordinary journey, we wind up at another skyline, where the force of the capacity to appreciate anyone on a deeper level enlightens our way forward. All through this excursion, we have investigated the huge oceans of the ability to understand people on a deeper level, finding its significant effect on both our own and proficient lives. Allow us now to embrace the insight we have acquired and headed out towards a future improved with the upgraded capacity to understand people on a deeper level.

Emotional intelligence illuminates our interactions and relationships, paving the way for genuine connections and understanding, like the guiding star that brightens the night sky. Embracing the impact of emotional intelligence on life and work By embracing the capacity to appreciate anyone on a deeper level in our lives, we develop mindfulness, self-guideline, sympathy, and interactive abilities, the actual quintessence of our profound compass.

Emotional intelligence propels us toward effective leadership, harmonious teamwork, and increased productivity in the workplace. We inspire those around us and foster a culture of empathy and cooperation as we navigate the complex waters of human emotions. Embracing a Satisfying and Tough Future with an Improved Capacity to understand individuals on a profound level

With the capacity to understand people on a profound level as our directing compass, we set forth toward a satisfying and strong future. As we develop the capacity to understand individuals on a profound level inside ourselves, we foster a profound comprehension of our feelings and the feelings of others.
We learn to handle difficulties in life with grace, to find courage in the face of them, and to see setbacks as opportunities for development.

Through sympathy and empathy, we sustain significant associations with others, encouraging a feeling of having a place and backing. With each experience, we leave a path of understanding and generosity, making waves of positive change in our general surroundings.

We discover the key to unlocking our hearts and minds' full potential in the embrace of emotional intelligence. As we explore the rhythmic movements of life, we do as such with realness and profound insight.

Together, we make an existence where sympathy, empathy, and the capacity to appreciate people on a deeper level thrive, and we praise the significant effect of understanding and close-to-home strength.

Allow us to proceed with this excursion with appreciation and assurance, realising that the journey of the capacity to understand people on a profound level is a persistent one, with vast open doors for development and disclosure.

As we sail into the future, let the floods of the capacity to understand individuals on a deeper level convey us toward a world loaded up with sympathy, intelligence, and profound strengthening. We can reach the shores of a life that is more compassionate, harmonious, and fulfilled by embracing the journey of emotional intelligence.